Dedini

MICROSOFT® PRESS

A MUCH, MUCH BETTER WORLD

PUBLISHED BY

Microsoft Press

A Division of Microsoft Corporation

10700 Northup Way, Box 97200, Bellevue, WA 98009

Library of Congress Cataloging in Publication Data
Dedini, Eldon, 1921 –
A much, much better world

1. Computers—Caricatures and cartoons.
2. American wit and humor, Pictorial. I. Title.
NC1429.D345A4   1985   741.5′973   85-4971

ISBN 0-914845-50-0

Distributed to the book trade
in the United States and Canada
by Simon & Schuster, Inc.

Simon and Schuster Order No. 0-671-55777-7

Distributed to the book trade outside the United States
and Canada by Penguin Books Ltd.

Penguin Books Ltd., Harmondsworth, Middlesex, England
Penguin Books Australia Ltd., Ringwood, Victoria, Australia
Penguin Books N.Z. Ltd., 182-190 Wairau Road,
Auckland 10, New Zealand

Penguin ISBN 0-14-087-143-8

British Cataloging in Publication Data available

Printed and bound in the United States of America.

1 2 3 4 5 6 7 8 9 FGFG 8 9 0 9 8 7 6 5

"Someday all these people will have personal computers, and it will be a much, much better world."

"And what's more, I'm even afraid of automated-teller machines!"

"Bravo, Santucci. For the first time I *really* feel organized."

"Software will save my people."

"I've learned things at my mother's knee, in my father's woodshed, behind the barn, and on the street—but *never* from floppy disks."

"From this point on, they've never seen a computer salesman."

"Extended Binary Coded Decimal Interchange Code,
Dynamic Storage Allocation,
Queued Indexed Sequential Access Method,
Fast Interline Nonactive Automatic Control...."

"A word of advice . . . there's a great deal of Artificial Intelligence in the head offices."

"When reaching for more K, beware of crashing head."

"INPUT 82
GOTO PAGEMILL
LEFT G5
IF G3 < > 57000
GOTO 280
EXIT."

"I'm putting all my memory into an XT 68000 so I won't lose it."

"This is not compatible with that, and that is not compatible with those, and those aren't compatible with these, and the new models aren't compatible with any of them—however, *I'm* compatible and I'll take care of you!"

"Is it progress to have solutions
to problems that don't exist?"

"We are most fortunate that our great Lenin gave us all the Artificial Intelligence
we'll ever need—pass it on."

Jabberdata

'Twas brillig, and the blithy bytes
Did frim and fimble in the NMOS:
All erlangs were elite Poisson,
And the modem moths cohabitate.

"Beware the Jabberdata, my son!
The maw that sucks, the claws that crunch!
Beware the ALPHANUM, and shun
The fructuous OUTWATS!"

And, as in cordless thought he stood,
The Jabberdata, yagi antenna aflame,
Came bussing toward the deadly embrace,
Glitching, glitching in its frame!

1011, 1100! 1101, 000111! 101011, 110110!
The digitals went igiti-igiti-ack!
He left it erased, and with its transmultiplexer
He went crossfooting back.

"And hast thou slain the Jabberdata?
Come to my arms, my nerdish boy!
O crapjous day! Harroo! Harray!"
Chortled he in processed joy.

'Twas brillig, and the blithy bytes,
Did frim and fimble in the night:
The erlangs modulated out of sight,
And von Neumann's ghost was galooping bright.

"Are they really compatible, and will they interface with the Kikuyu?"

"Company ahead of its time with faulty software needs unlisted 800 number."

"I'd meet him at the door with
two martinis and a sexy dress.
Didn't do a bit of good.
So I started using his computer,
and now they call me Modem Molly.
I've made conquests in fourteen states,
including Puerto Rico."

Dedini

"Mr. McFadden will be tied up the rest of the day, but you can talk to our computer if you'd like."

"The computer was down today. We have no Fagioli Toscanelli al Vino Bianco."

What if Freud had had a computer?

"We merged with a Japanese company."

"Lemonade is slow, but I'm making a mint tutoring all the dads on the block."

Friendly Software

"Checking for illegals. What else?"

"It's harassment in the workplace. This robot keeps reaching over
and loosening his neighbor's nuts."

Portrait of Interactivity

"You were warned *never* to open your Macintosh!"

"Universe gets bigger as chips get smaller."

"I know how much you hate costume parties, dear—why don't you stay home with your software."

"Good morning, ma'am. We were just passing by, a bit bored with hiking, and we
wondered if you had a PC or something compatible."

"By golly, that friggin' bank stuck it to me again!"

"Probably just another traveling salesman."

"Better join us, Rico. We're the first on the street to use computers."

"Someday all this will be done by computer."

Milton Moffet has spent the last two years in his garage developing a program to transmigrate souls to outer space. Says Milton, "I think my code's coming around. Last week my garage jumped from 724 to 812 Ripple Avenue."

Milton Moffet, Interview
Cupertino Times, 4/7/85

When things go wrong, where to look...

Look in the back.

Look at the ceiling.

Look at your shoes.

Look in your wallet.

"Still compatible with people after 5000 years."

"This is Lydia on the tenth floor. I just cracked their accounting system and we can ask for a buck-fifty raise with no sweat come contract time."

"It was Tuesday night, late.
The Federal Government's computer
hacked into *my* PC and asked
for ideas on how to solve
the budget deficit!"

"Don't look now, but I think we're being accessed."

"Emperor has no clothes—but selling them anyway to VaporSoft, MicroOz, Windware, and MegaMind."

"Hazel, help me! I can't find my cubbyhole."

"Sonny forgives you, dear. His computer company is now grossing
$200,000 a week, but he thinks he understands why you were
against putting any of your money into it."

"Always hide the password
in plain sight."

MacGogh

"Tell me again . . . which Soft are you? Micro, Meta, Super, Inter, or Future?"

Carnal Memories

"Hey, Bella! Have *I* got a program for you!"

"He hasn't spoken to me for weeks...and yesterday he left an insulting drawing of me on his computer."

"Don't curse the darkness; check your warranty."

"These are expansion chips for the updated version of the universe."

"But John, you *promised* I wouldn't become just another peripheral."

"It's a placebo. But it's curing his fear of computers."

"Unlimited visions are an illusion to the limited."

"This is *not* a good time to ask me how I like my new computer. This morning I told it I wanted the best airline reservation to Atlanta and it booked me on Dip 'n Dash Airways by way of Peoria. Then I asked it for a recipe for Chicken Tetrazzini and it fed me a low-cal Chicken à la King instead. But the real kicker came when I asked it to analyze the company's financial position, and it told me I had just lost my shirt!"

"When making quantum leaps, check with patent office
before jumping into market."

"You don't need to know anything about computers to really enjoy me."

"Finally, at 3 a.m. I discovered the password and logged in. Then the computer told me there were four hackers ahead of me and put me on hold."

"I love your printouts, Blanchford. They lie like hell!"

"Remember, I can *always* unplug you!"

"I was running this proposal,
editing from a pull-down menu
using a mouse and entering data
from the spreadsheets, when the
manager busts in and he *knows*
I have only 64K, but right off the bat
he shouts, 'What the hell is this?'—
Well, he's a micro-brain and doesn't
know his CMOS from his NMOS,
so we have this interface,
and I explode...."

"It's lovely when the night falls dark and deep and the home computers come on."

"Don't quote me, but I've heard him called the Nanosecond Man."

"Geez, Pop, *you* must have seen what *I* saw on the Bulletin Board tonight."

"Now that we know we are God's software, how is your program coming along?"

"Think back . . . which keys did you press?"

"Is there *really* enough data
to feed 1,000,000,000
desk top computers?"

"First, I found it difficult to discuss sex with my kids; now, I find it difficult to discuss computers with them...."

"In 1972, this answer would have taken 783 pounds of chalk
and 32 acres of blackboard."

"He who flees from High Tech, forfeits chance for windfall profits."

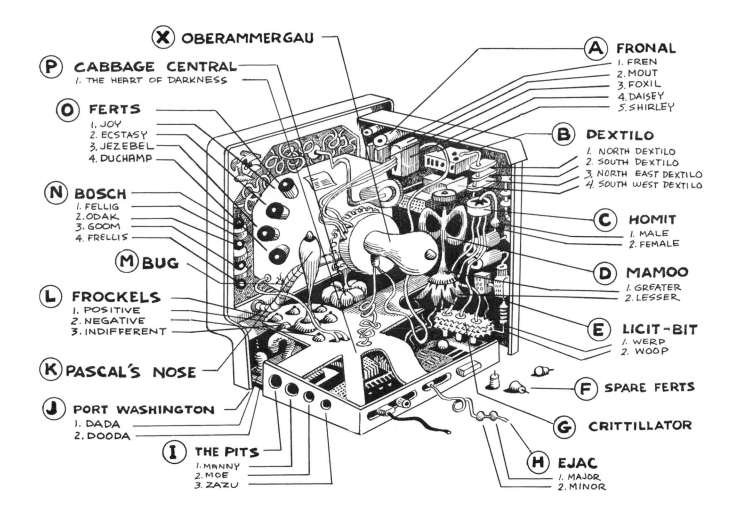

(X) OBERAMMERGAU

(P) CABBAGE CENTRAL
1. THE HEART OF DARKNESS

(O) FERTS
1. JOY
2. ECSTASY
3. JEZEBEL
4. DUCHAMP

(N) BOSCH
1. FELLIG
2. ODAK
3. GOOM
4. FRELLIS

(M) BUG

(L) FROCKELS
1. POSITIVE
2. NEGATIVE
3. INDIFFERENT

(K) PASCAL'S NOSE

(J) PORT WASHINGTON
1. DADA
2. DOODA

(I) THE PITS
1. MANNY
2. MOE
3. ZAZU

(A) FRONAL
1. FREN
2. MOUT
3. FOXIL
4. DAISEY
5. SHIRLEY

(B) DEXTILO
1. NORTH DEXTILO
2. SOUTH DEXTILO
3. NORTH EAST DEXTILO
4. SOUTH WEST DEXTILO

(C) HOMIT
1. MALE
2. FEMALE

(D) MAMOO
1. GREATER
2. LESSER

(E) LICIT-BIT
1. WERP
2. WOOP

(F) SPARE FERTS

(G) CRITTILLATOR

(H) EJAC
1. MAJOR
2. MINOR

There's always more to learn.

INPUT B   HIT JUMP
GOTO POOL END   SPLASH CRASH
CIRCLE SPEED 66   APPLAUSE
REPEAT 66   REWARD TWO FISH

"You're right. It *is* a great wine!"

"I'm curious. Is this a computer date?"

"Look deep into your screen—reflect on the chip... we are on the cusp of an intelligence that no one knows exists. Languages no one yet speaks, ideas no one can understand. It's our only hope."

Ogden Munroe, Guest Speaker
Santa Cruz, June 1984

さあ出てこい！　あんなマニァゥルを書いたのはどこのどいつだ？

("All right, who the hell wrote that manual?")

Portrait of a Computer Widow

"Look...the whole human comedy on one chip!"

Man beginning to understand his life through a personal computer.

"Yes, your divorce is very sad, but the good news is that it's largely boilerplate and my fee will be nominal."

"It's the instant answers I find hardest to deal with."

"I want to thank my mother, my father, my wife, my board of directors, and all the robots down at the plant."

"Oh John. Not *another* six-pack of software!"

"It's the new PRUNE XT made in Albania. Copied from the APPLE 2 and the APRICOT 3, and their earlier model, the FIG 1."

The miracle is that all 4 billion 83 million of us fit somewhere into a computer.

"Oh, do you sell data? I'll probably need some of that too."

"Your carburetor's way off. Your valves are so-so. Your VISA balance is just fine."

"You have just accessed the Big Dynamo-Data computer in Chicago. Your number has been turned over to our Enforcer Department. Exit immediately or you'll be the victim of a humongous power surge that will make our day."

"That's what I like about you, Fred. The way you tackle the raw data, process it, and get on with life."

"Three computers in this family *has* created a lot of stress, but if we got a multiplexer that operated a number of I/O devices simultaneously interleaving two or more activities and distributing events by networking those interleaved sequences to the respective activities, we'd all be happier."

"While it's still fresh, let me enter all this gossip in my portable PC."

"Nuts to this sandpile! I'm going in and work with my computer."

"If we keep at this we could become rich kids. At the very worst, rich old men."

"The line moves perceptibly faster with computerization."

Award-winning cartoonist Eldon Dedini's career has spanned
more than four decades. A native of King City, California, Dedini graduated
from Chouinard Art Institute in Los Angeles. He began his professional career as a
cartoonist for the *Salinas Morning Post* (now the *Salinas Californian*) before moving on
to work at Walt Disney Studios. From 1946 to 1950, he was a member of the staff at
Esquire magazine. Dedini then went to work for *The New Yorker*, where he
has been a contract cartoonist for many years. He is currently also a
contract cartoonist for *Playboy*. On three occasions Dedini has
been honored with the Best Magazine Cartoonist Award from the
National Cartoonists Society. His work has also appeared in
Punch, Colliers, Look, Holiday, the *Saturday Evening Post,*
and *Sports Illustrated.* Eldon Dedini
resides in Carmel, California.

Cover illustration by Dedini
Cover design by Karen-Lynne de Robinson
Text composition by Microsoft Press in Baskerville, using the CCI
composition system and the Mergenthaler Linotron 202
digital phototypesetter.

Cover printed on 12 pt. Carolina by Philips Offset Company, Inc., Mamaroneck, N.Y.
Text stock, 60 lb. Glatfelter Offset, supplied by Carpenter/Offutt.
Book printed and bound by Fairfield Graphics,
Fairfield, Pennsylvania.